CHARLI

KOOL-1

Illustrations: Jette Jørgensen

Charles Ferro:
Kool-1
Teen Readers, Level 3

Series editors: Ulla Malmmose
and Charlotte Bistrup

Cover: Mette Plesner
Photo: Simon Podgorsek/iStock

Copyright © 2002 Charles Ferro and
EASY READERS, Copenhagen
- a subsidiary of Lindhardt og Ringhof Forlag A/S,
an Egmont company.

ISBN Denmark 978-87-23-90830-8
www.easyreaders.eu

The CEFR levels stated on the back of the book
are approximate levels.

Easy Readers

EGMONT

Printed in Denmark

About the author

Charles Ferro was born in Utica, a mediumsized city in upstate New York. He holds a Bachelor of Business Administration degree from St. John Fisher College, and earned a certificate for the teaching of English at the State University of New York. Currently a free-lance writer and journalist.

Charles Ferro has been living in Denmark since 1977 with his wife Rita. They have a daughter, Maria Celeste. Charles enjoys reading, fishing and cooking.

When he was around nine years old, he asked his grandmother to take him to a movie made from an Edgar Allan Poe story. Since then he has loved stories about the supernatural.

About writing Charles Ferro says, "Part of my brain is still fourteen years old and doing books for kids is an excellent means of reviling part of my life – things that did happen and lies about what never happened."

Two boys, one birthday

Brent Scialfa and Trey Striker were born on the same day 16 years ago. Their birthday, May 10, was really the only thing they had in common. Brent was born in Port Mohawk, a little city in New York State, and Trey was born in Houston, Texas. They were both happy little babies, but by the time Trey was five, he had forgotten how to smile. Brent, however, smiled a lot. In fact, he was known for his smile. The girls in Rutgers High School really liked his smile, even some of the older girls in his sister Karen's class.

Karen was one year ahead of Brent in school and she really acted like an older sister. They were like cat and dog at home, where they lived with their father who worked as a *carpenter*, building houses. Brent and Karen lost their mother in a car accident when he was 12 and she was 13. It was a very hard time for the three of them, and Brent didn't smile for a long time. But things got better in time. Brent's smile returned. Their father, Jim, went to work every day and did his best to make a good home for his two children.

Karen became the woman of the house and gave Brent a lot of jobs to do. He hated to be told what to do, but his father had said, "Your sister knows how to run a house better than either of us. So, do what she tells you to do." The worst job was hanging clothes out to dry when the weather was good. Sometimes Brent's friends would see him hanging clothes. "Hey Brent, when you're finished you can come over to my house and hang up our clothes," Billy Falk called to him one

| *carpenter*, person who makes things from wood

day. Brent raced over to Billy and the two 14-year-olds got into a terrible fight. Billy won, but for some reason they became good friends after that, best friends.

Brent told his father he would do anything if he didn't have to hang clothes any more. Jim's reply was, "I don't like to wash and dry dishes, go grocery shopping, clean the bathroom and a lot of other things, but I do them." There was nothing more to talk about and Brent got used to hanging clothes. The funny thing was that Billy helped him do it a few times.

Karen knew how Brent felt about hanging up clothes, so she washed clothes at least twice a week. And the two of them would fight. "It's a good thing I'm a carpenter," their father would say. "Because one day you two are going to tear the house down and I'll have to build a new one."

Brent never hit her – even though she often tried to

hit him – but he knew how to do something even better. He would hold her arms with one hand and wrap his legs around hers so she couldn't kick, and then he would almost touch her *belly button*. Karen hated to have her belly button touched. She would scream and try to bite him, but Brent was much stronger. He would hold his finger over her belly button and say, "Belly button check. Let's see who has a belly button."

After a while he would let her go, but first he would make her promise that she wouldn't hit him. Brent would let her go, and then run for his life.

So they really were cat and dog, but like many cats and dogs they learned to live together under the same roof. What was more important, they were both happy and their father was a happy man. The three of them lived and worked together as a family.
Trey Striker's life was completely different.

Bobby Striker, Trey's father, and Marcy Belmont met in a department store where they had both gone to steal things. It was love at first sight. They worked well together, stealing things and selling them for money. It was easy.

Around a year later they had a child they named Trey. He was a beautiful baby, but Bobby and Marcy

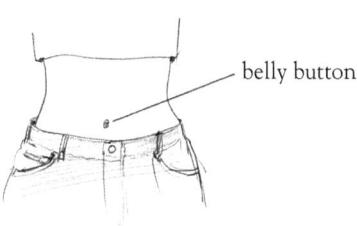

paid little attention to him as he grew. They did find the time to hit him if he cried, or if he said he was hungry. That's why he stopped smiling around the time he was five.

As he got older they had even less time; they were too busy "working." Trey remembered how people would come to their home and buy little packages from his mother or father. He didn't know then what was in the little packages.

Trey learned to find food in the house, usually just bread or he would eat the last pieces of cold pizza after his parents had eaten the best part. When he was old enough to go to school, he learned how to walk into a store and walk out with things he never paid for. It was the only way he could put food in his stomach, but he also stole clothes and the things other kids in school had.

Trey went to seven different schools as he was growing up. His parents moved from town to town, because they had to stay one step ahead of the police. Trey learned things in school, but not always what the teachers were teaching. He learned to ask other boys, "Let me hold your lunch money." The other boys were afraid of Trey, so they gave him money and he would have money to buy lunch at the school cafeteria.

Trey also learned to sign his mother's or father's name to papers he had to give to the teachers. It was easy. He learned how to get bigger and better things for himself. All he had to do was take things. And he did this without ever thinking that it could be wrong. In fact, he believed it was the only way to do it.

When Trey was 14 his life changed. Bobby and Marcy went to prison for doing something so horrible, the newspapers would not even write about it. Trey was suddenly all alone, but he did not care. What did worry him was that the city *officials* would try to find a home for him. So Trey went away.

He *hitched* rides around the country. Sometimes he would steal some money, or something he could sell for money from the people who gave him the rides. He stole from stores, cars and other places. He went to Los Angeles for a while, then to Chicago and a lot of smaller towns in between. Trey met people and learned a lot of ways to make money. Stealing cars was an easy way to make money, and Trey learned how to drive at the same time. It was easy for him, because he never thought he was doing anything wrong.

Trey arrived in New York City on his 16th birthday. He soon met people he could use to help him make money, and he learned a lot from them. Other kids tried to live on the streets, but most of them didn't make it. Trey was tough. You see, you become tough when you get hit a lot and Trey was used to being hit for as long as he could remember.

One important thing he learned was to get false ID cards. Trey had three drivers' licenses, each with his picture and a false name. If the police ever asked questions, he could just show them one of the licenses. It was as easy as that.

One day he met some young men who were selling pills called Kool-1. Trey found this was a very easy way to make money. All he had to do was buy a few pills for $4 each and sell them for $10. He bought them from a

officials, people who have important jobs in government or companies
hitch, to stand in the road to get a ride

man called Sway, who bought them from The Professor, the man who made Kool-1. Trey sold them at schools and clubs where youngsters went to dance in a small town in New Jersey, just across the river from New York City.

But Trey knew that he was taking the risk of getting caught by the police. So, he met some kids from a few schools and let them do the selling. All Trey had to do was sell Kool-1 pills to them and count his money. And one thing he never, never did – he never tried to take Kool-1 himself. Trey knew that some kids had died from Kool-1, but that wasn't his problem. Nobody had forced them to eat the pills. The problem for him was this: Every time some stupid kid died, the police worked extra hard to find the sellers of Kool-1 and that was bad for Trey's business.

He found new schools and new clubs where he could do business. The only problem was that other people were selling at those schools and clubs. When Trey tried to start selling at High St. School a man named The Bear told Trey that it was his area. If Trey didn't go away, The Bear would hurt him. Trey agreed to find another place, but one week later The Bear "disappeared" and High St. School was Trey's. The same thing happened to other sellers if they got in Trey's way and one day Sway disappeared, so Trey began buying the pills from The Professor for less than one dollar.

Trey had a *web* of people working for him. Once a week he would collect his money. He made a mountain of money, but it wasn't enough. Trey thought about bringing his business to New York City where there

| *web*, a lot of

was a lot of money and a lot of places to sell Kool-1. But he was smart enough to know that he wasn't big enough yet. New York had some really big sellers who had more people working for them than Trey did. It was too dangerous.

Trey thought about it for a few days and decided to take his business to Port Mohawk, a city around 400 kilometers northwest of New York. His workers would continue to earn money at the old places while Trey started a new business. He figured that once a week he would come back to the town near New York City to collect his money and get a fresh supply of Kool-1 from The Professor. After Port Mohawk there were other cities and towns where people would be happy to do business with him. There was Kingston, Albany, Troy, Amsterdam, Utica, Syracuse, Geneva. His business would get bigger and bigger, just like a big company.

Welcome to Port Mohawk

Trey knew he would need a car, so he asked one of his sellers – a woman who was 22 years old – to buy the car in her name. He gave the woman a couple of hundred dollars and a little bag of Kool-1. She paid more than $30,000 cash for the car and nobody asked any questions.

So Trey got into his car and headed for Port Mohawk. The first three nights he spent in a motel outside of town. Every day he would buy the newspaper so he could find a place to live. On the second day he found exactly what he was looking for.

Trey figured the best way to get started was to go to

where there would be customers for Kool-1. So he found a school. A few days later he was the new pupil in Rutgers High School. It was easy. He had arrived in town just a couple of weeks after the new school year
5 started. Trey wrote a letter and signed his mother's and father's names at the bottom. He brought the letter to the school and explained that his parents could not come with him because they were working. It was as easy as that.

10 Brent Scialfa watched as his English teacher Mr. McMahon introduced the "new student" to the 10th grade class. The boys looked at him and wondered if he could play baseball or basketball or football. Some of the girls *giggled* and whispered to each other. Brent
15 thought that the new kid looked like any other kid except for one thing that made the hairs on Brent's arms tickle. The kid's eyes. The new kid's eyes reminded Brent of a *shark*. But Brent didn't think too much about it.

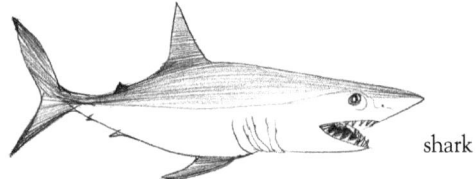
shark

20 Mr. McMahon gave Trey a couple of books and asked him to sit in an empty seat next to Brent. Trey walked to the seat and sat down. Brent turned to him and smiled, as if to say, "Welcome to Rutgers High." Trey nodded, but didn't smile.
25 After 45 minutes the school bell rang and the stu-

| *giggle*, a silly way of laughing

dents headed for their next class. Billy Falk grabbed Brent's arm and said, "Should we ask the new kid if he wants to play basketball after class?" Brent said, "OK", so they walked up to Trey in the hall.

"Hey, I'm Billy Falk. This is Brent Scialfa," Billy said, holding out his hand. Trey shook Billy's hand, and then Brent's. As Trey said, "Hi," Brent felt as if Trey was studying him, like he was trying to learn more by looking at him.

"We're going to play basketball after school. Do you want to join us?" Billy asked.

"Ah, no thanks," Trey answered. "I can't play. I hurt my knee at my old school." Lies were just as easy to tell as the truth.

Brent looked at Trey. He noticed a little *scar* on Trey's cheek and that one of his eyebrows was swollen – like a boxer's. Brent saw that the clothes Trey was wearing were expensive, and the one thing that seemed very unusual was that Trey didn't smile. He wasn't unfriendly, but he wasn't really friendly either.

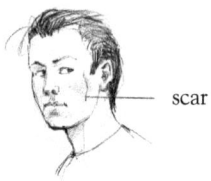

scar

"Where do you live," Billy asked him.

"I live with my parents out on Steuben Road," Trey replied. The answer sounded odd to Brent. Why hadn't Trey just said, "I live on Steuben Road," instead of, "I live with my parents on Steuben Road?" That's the way Brent would have said it.

"Wow, that's far away. How do you get to school? Do you take the bus?" Billy asked.

"No, my father drops me off on his way to work."

The truth was, Trey drove his car into town and parked it on a quiet street. He walked to school from there. The house on Steuben Road was a 20-minute drive from town, but Trey had been careful to choose that house. It was in a wooded area surrounded by farms. The closest neighbor was a five-minute walk away, so nobody would notice that Trey lived there alone.

But Billy's question made Trey start to think. His car

was brand new. It wasn't a fancy car, but it wasn't the kind of car a 16-year-old high school student would drive either. "Ah, my father drops me off, but I'm going to buy a car with some money I saved up from working," he said. In two days Trey would buy an old car that he could drive back and forth to school. That would be easy enough. He could buy an old car himself without anybody asking questions. Trey figured he could drive the new car, when he went back to the New York City area.

"Oh, where did you work?"

"This kid asks a lot of questions," Trey thought. "Too many questions." At the same time, Trey realized he would have to have a lot of answers to a lot of questions. "I used to work at a drug store," he said. "We lived in a town just outside New York City."

"Hey, you guys, I have to get going to History class," Brent said. "Maybe we'll see you later, Trey."

"Yeah," Trey answered. "Hey, where's Room 222? Remember I'm new here."

"Come on," Billy said. "I have to go to Math class in Room 224. Follow me."

Trey could already see that Billy was going to help him start his business in Port Mohawk. Life on the streets had taught Trey a lot about people. Some people were easy to *persuade*, others were not so easy. Billy was one of the easy ones.

Brent walked down the hall in the other direction. For some reason he looked over his shoulder and saw Billy walking beside Trey. Brent didn't know why, but he didn't like what he saw.

| *persuade*, [pə'sweid] to change a person's mind

15

Artie Flowers

It only took Trey a few weeks to become popular in school. The girls liked him, because he was good-looking and charming. The boys liked him because he told good stories about New York City, and he would drive around with them in his new – although it was really 10 years old – car. Billy always seemed to be the one to sit in the front seat with Trey. Brent spent quite a bit of time with Trey and Billy, but he was beginning to see that the more time he spent with Trey, the less time he spent playing basketball or doing the other things he used to do with Billy. And all the boys were a little bit afraid of Trey, especially after he almost got into a fight with Lee Torp.

Lee was the toughest boy in Rutgers High School. In fact, he was the school *bully*. He was a year older than Brent and was in the same class as Karen. One morning Brent, Billy, Trey and some other guys were standing outside the school building waiting for the bell to ring. Billy turned to Trey and asked, "Hey Trey, can I borrow five *bucks* until Tuesday?" Trey pulled some folded bills out of his pocket and gave a five-dollar bill to Billy, who put it in his own pocket. Trey always had money with him, not a lot, but sometimes as much as 40 dollars.

Lee Torp stood nearby with some of his friends and saw Trey putting the money back into his pocket. Lee turned to his friends and said, "Watch this," and walked toward Trey. The smile on Lee's face meant trouble.

> *bully*, a big person who often hurts a smaller person
> *bucks*, slang for dollars

"Hey Trey, let me have ten dollars until next week," Lee said.

Trey looked him straight in the eye and answered, "I don't have any money." Brent, Billy and their friends took a step back.

"I just saw you put a handful of bills in your pocket," Lee said, taking another step toward him. Trey didn't move and his eyes were cold as ice.

"I don't have any money," Trey repeated in a flat voice. He didn't move, but Brent noticed that Trey's whole body seemed ready for action.

Lee wasn't used to having anybody stand up to him. He hardly knew what to say. "Oh, I thought I saw money. I just wanted to borrow ten until next week."

Trey shook his head slowly to say no. Lee nodded his head, and went back to his friends.

"Wow," Billy said, as Lee walked away. "I never saw Lee act like that before. He usually starts a fight before the other guy even knows he's in a fight." Trey was silent.

Just then, the bell rang and everyone entered the building. Billy walked beside Trey. He felt good walking beside him. It made him feel important.

And Billy was the first one to try Kool-1. It was on the Friday night after Trey and Lee almost got into a fight. Trey and Billy were in Artie Flowers' place. Artie was a man of around 30 who sold newspapers, magazines and a few other things, but he had a lot of video games and other machines. A lot of the kids from school would meet there.

Trey had gotten Artie Flowers' name from The Professor. He had paid Artie a visit the day after he arrived in Port Mohawk. "Do you want to make some easy money?" Trey had asked him. The one thing Artie liked better than money was easy money, so he listened to the boy. In just a few minutes, Artie and Trey were doing business. It was simple. Trey told Artie where he could pick up a bag of pills once a week and where Artie could drop off the money when the pills were sold. It was perfect. Artie knew a lot of people, and lots of kids went to Artie's place.

So, on Friday night Billy and Trey walked into Artie Flowers place. Billy said hello to Artie Flowers, who was standing behind the *counter* reading a magazine. Artie just nodded his head as he usually did when one of the kids said hello to him. What surprised Billy was that Artie said, "Hey Trey, how's it going?" Trey nodded his head at Artie and looked around to see who was there. Billy headed for his favorite video game and put some money into it. Trey sat at the machine beside him and played another game.

After playing for an hour or so, Billy said to Trey, "There's not much happening here. I understand why Brent didn't want to go out tonight. Not many kids are out tonight and there isn't a single girl in here."

"Yeah, it's not very exciting," Trey answered.

"I think I'll go home and see if there's a movie on TV," Billy said. "I'm tired anyway."

Trey looked at him for a second and realized this was the chance he was looking for. "Stick around for a while," he said. "I think Artie might have something for you so you won't feel so tired." Billy looked at him, but didn't understand what Trey meant.

Trey walked up to Artie who was removing money from one of the machines. The *coins* dumped out of the machine into a bag Artie held. Trey said something to

counter

coins

Artie, and Artie looked over at Billy. He nodded and Trey walked back to where Billy sat.

Trey handed Billy some coins and said, "Get yourself a soda and then go see Artie. He has something that will make you feel better."

Billy tried to say something, but Trey moved his head to one side, telling Billy to go.

Billy walked to the soda machine, put some money in and pushed a button. He picked up the soda, but didn't open it. Artie Flowers watched as Billy walked toward him. "Trey told me you ...." Billy started to say, but Artie looked down at something on the counter. Billy's eyes followed his. There was a little blue pill beside Artie's hand. Billy could see the word Kool-1 on the pill. He started to say something, but Artie moved his head as if to say, "Take it and get out of here."

With the little pill in his hand, Billy went back to Trey. Billy looked around to be sure nobody was looking and then opened his hand to show Trey the pill. Trey nodded.

"This isn't ecstasy is it?" Billy asked.

"No, no, don't worry. It's just a little something that will give you more energy," Trey answered. "You know, like those energy drinks they sell. You can buy them in the soda machine." Trey pointed to the machine where Billy had just bought the soda.

Billy seemed to be afraid. "I'll tell you what," Trey said. "Give me half and we'll have a good time." He held his hand out. Billy looked around and placed the Kool-1 pill in Trey's hand.

Trey took the pill and bit it in half. He put the other half in Billy's hand and took the soda from him. Before he took a drink of soda, Trey moved his tongue and put the half pill between his teeth and cheek so he wouldn't swallow it. He took a big drink of the soda and handed it back to Billy, who put the other half of the pill in his mouth and swallowed it with soda.

"In just a little while we'll both be smiling," Trey said. "Let's go take a ride."

Just before they walked out the door, Trey nodded at Artie and he nodded back. "There's more where that came from," Artie said to Billy.

The two of them walked toward Trey's car. Trey unlocked the door and sat behind the wheel. Just before he closed the door, he spit the Kool-1 into the street.

Billy got into the car not knowing what to expect, but he would soon be taking a ride he would never forget.

Billy the salesman

On Saturday morning, Brent and a few other boys met at school to play basketball on the outdoor court in the schoolyard. It was a warm day for mid-October and a few of the boys had taken off their T-shirts after the first game.

Brent couldn't understand why Billy wasn't there. They always met at noon to play on Saturdays when the weather was good. Billy finally showed up just before two o'clock, but many of the boys had already left by then. Brent was playing two-on-two with three others when Billy arrived. "Where have you been?" Brent asked him.

"I slept late. Sorry," Billy answered. "I have to tell you something when you finish playing." He sat down on the ground in a circle of sunlight to watch his friends play.

Brent and the other three finished their game in a few minutes. The other boys gathered their things and said good-bye. Brent walked over to Billy.

"You wouldn't believe what happened last night," Billy started. "I went to Artie Flowers' with Trey, …" Billy began, and told Brent all about Kool-1.

The first thing Brent said was, "You're crazy. That stuff could be dangerous." But Billy repeated what Trey had told him – that it was like an energy drink, and that it wasn't dangerous at all. Trey had said that it wasn't illegal, but told Billy to be careful about who he told, because it wasn't really legal either.

"It's about the same as drinking beer. Lots of kids who are too young drink beer and beer is not illegal. It's only illegal for us, because we're too young," Billy said. "But this Kool-1 is a million times better. You've got to try it."

Billy told Brent about how much he had laughed the night before, and about how much energy Kool-1 had given him. In fact, he still had a lot of energy when he went to bed and hadn't fallen asleep until around four in the morning. He told him about how Trey had picked up a couple of girls and how they had driven around town having a great time. Brent listened, and it all really didn't sound too bad.

"And the best thing is this," Billy said. "Trey seems to know Artie Flowers, and he says that we can buy the stuff from Artie for a few dollars if we buy a lot of the pills. I mean if we buy 15 or 20 of them at a time."

"Are you sure this stuff isn't ecstasy, just with a different name?" Brent asked.

"No, no. It's completely different," Billy answered. "This stuff is Kool-1 and it's almost legal. And think about it – Trey says the stuff costs ten dollars a pill in New York. If we buy a lot it will only cost five dollars and we can sell it for ten and make five dollars."

"I don't know, Billy. It just sounds wrong," Brent said.

"Look at me. It didn't hurt me," Billy said, holding out his arms to show he was in fine shape. "Does it look as if it has done anything bad to me?"

"No, you look just as stupid as you always did," Brent laughed.

"Listen. Tonight there will be a dance at school. Let's get some guys together and take some Kool-1. It will be fun," Billy said. "I've got enough money to buy around ten pills. I can sell them to the other guys. I don't have to sell them for ten dollars – maybe just eight. But don't tell them what I pay for them."

"I don't know, Billy."

"Come on. Don't be such a chicken. It's not going to hurt you. Try it once and if you don't like it you never have to try it again."

"We'll see what happens," Brent answered. "I'll meet you outside the dance at seven-thirty, OK?"

"OK. See you then."

They walked together for a while, then each headed home. Brent thought about what Billy had told him. Part of him was afraid, but another part of him wanted to try Kool-1. He wasn't sure what to do.

Billy went home and watched some television before he ate dinner with his parents and two younger brothers. He called a few of his friends and told them about Kool-1 before he left the house early to do business with Artie Flowers.

Artie knew what Billy wanted as soon as he walked through the door. "What can I do for you?" Artie said to him.

Billy was afraid. His hands were wet and he could hardly talk. "Can I .. ah .. can I get ..."

Artie stopped him. "I've got ten great video games for fifty dollars. Pay now and go outside and wait on the corner." He held his hand out for the money. At first Billy didn't know what Artie meant when he had said "ten video games," but it only took a second to figure it out. So, he dug into his pocket and took out a twenty and three tens and put the bills on the counter. Artie folded the money and put it into his shirt pocket. Billy waited, but Artie looked at him without blinking, until he *jerked* his thumb over his shoulder, telling Billy to go.

As Billy walked outside, Artie took his *cell phone* and pushed some numbers. Billy waited on the corner outside Artie Flowers' place. He wondered if Artie was going to keep the money and that was the end of that. But after around 10 minutes a woman with fire-red hair walked up to him. Her lips were painted red and she had a lot of green make-up above her eyes. She wore a

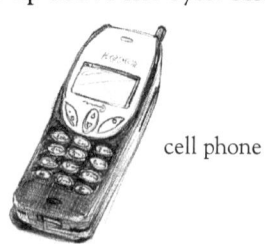

cell phone

to jerk, to move quickly

gold ring in her eyebrow and the top of her shirt covered part of a home-made tattoo. It was Janie Rolien, Artie Flowers' girlfriend. "Nice night," she said to Billy, stepping close to him.

Billy smelled her perfume. She looked at him with a smile. "You're cute," she whispered, putting a finger on Billy's lower lip. His face turned as red as her lips and words wouldn't come out of his mouth. Janie lifted one eyebrow and then walked away. Billy didn't know what to say or do. He turned to her with his mouth open, but she just looked over her shoulder for a second. Billy thought she was looking at his feet, so he looked down at his feet. Beside his left shoe was a little brown envelope. He bent to pick it up and felt the pills inside the envelope. Quickly, Billy put it into his jacket pocket and headed for school to meet Brent and the other guys before the dance.

Billy looked over his shoulder every few seconds as he walked. It only took a few minutes to get to school, and his friends were waiting for him. Brent and some of the guys they played basketball with were there along with a couple of others. Margot Wicks, one of the girls from class, was there too. They all seemed excited.

"And what do you have for us?" Margot asked. She and the others formed a circle around Billy. He looked around first, and then took the envelope out of his pocket.

"Here it is, Kool-1 the one for fun," Billy said with a big smile. "Eight bucks and you'll have the time of your life."

Brent was the first to hand his money to Billy and the others followed. There were eight of them and they all swallowed the Kool-1 pills together. They looked at each other. Some of them looked a little scared, others kept a cool look on their faces. They didn't know what to expect.

"Let me have the other two pills, " Margot said to Billy. "Louise and Tina want to try it too."

"Remember to get eight bucks from each of them," Billy told her as he handed Margot the pills.

Trey came to the dance around 90 minutes later. He drove in from Utica where he had been doing business with someone he knew there. In other towns around Port Mohawk, other youngsters were gathering at dances or parties where Kool-1 would be the star. Trey didn't waste any time. He always remembered what a man in New York City had told him, "Get in fast, and get out fast if you have to."

Kool-1 rules

The dance in October was the start of Kool-1's popularity. Ten kids had taken it. They had a great time at the dance, having fun with their friends and enjoying the music. A couple of them were asked by their friends, "Why are you so happy tonight?" Some of them told their friends why they were so happy.

Other kids in Port Mohawk heard about Kool-1 from their friends and would try it on a Friday or Saturday night. Billy would go to Artie Flowers and buy as many as 25 pills for a weekend. Now he didn't even try to say anything to Janie Rolien. He would stand on the corner; she would walk by and drop an envelope of pills. Other boys and girls would do the same thing.

The situation was the same in the towns and cities

around Port Mohawk. By *Halloween*, at the end of
October, Trey was making ten thousand dollars a week.
He missed the big city, but Trey knew it was important
to act like a high school student for some time. It was
part of making money. Billy was happy, too, because he
was making almost a hundred on a weekend.

Every year Rutgers High School held a Halloween
dance and nearly all the kids in school would come.
They dressed up in costumes and the Halloween dance
was probably the biggest thing to happen all year.

Brent, Billy and their friends made plans for the
dance and of course Kool-1 was part of the plans. Billy
dressed up as Frankenstein's monster and went by Artie
Flowers to pick up 30 Kool-1 pills. He had never
bought so many before. Billy did not wear the Frankenstein mask as he waited for Janie Rolien, but he felt odd
standing there dressed in torn clothes and big boots.

"There you go, Frankie," Janie said, as she dropped
an envelope and walked past him. Billy thought she
could be going to a Halloween party with all the make-up she had on her face.

In a few minutes, Billy was standing outside school
doing business. He didn't want 30 kids standing in line
waiting to buy the Kool-1 from him, so he would sell
five or six pills to one kid who would then give them to
his or her friends. A lot of kids had already paid him at
school the day before. When he had finished, he joined
his friends.

Brent was standing with a group of boys and girls
dressed in different costumes. They were laughing at
something Trey had just said. Trey often didn't go out

Halloween, a Christian holiday, October 31.

on weekends; he often told Brent and the others that he had to do something with his parents. Tonight he was dressed up as Dracula. Everybody laughed at what Trey had said except him, but the vampire teeth he was wearing almost made it look as if he were smiling.

Billy came to them and held his hand out. "Here's your candy, kiddies," he said, holding out his hand with Kool-1 pills in it. Each of them took a pill and Billy put the last one into his mouth.

They passed around a bottle of soda to swallow the Kool-1. Brent – who was dressed as Spiderman – watched Trey as he put a pill into his mouth. He noticed how Trey moved his tongue inside his mouth until there was a little lump under his lip. Brent watched as Trey swallowed a mouthful of soda, but the little lump was still under his lip. "He didn't take the pill!" Brent thought to himself.

The group began to walk toward the door of the school building. Trey was a few steps behind the others. Brent looked at the glass on the door where he could see himself and some of the others as if he were looking in a mirror. His eyes went to Trey. Brent watched as Trey quickly put a hand to his mouth and then *tossed* something over his shoulder. "He threw the pill away!" Brent thought. He couldn't understand it and what he had just seen made Brent feel uncomfortable. There was something about Trey he didn't like, but he didn't know what.

Colored lights hung on the walls of the school *gymnasium*, and a DJ was on the stage playing music. Some people were dancing near the stage, but most of the kids stood in groups of five or six. Everyone was dressed in costumes, even the teachers who were there. There were around 300 kids at the dance, and around 100 of them had taken Kool-1.

Brent and Billy stood together talking. Next to them, Trey talked to a couple of boys. Brent looked around and saw his sister Karen standing with her girlfriends. One of them was Tif Creetan. Brent spotted Tif and got a feeling inside. At first he thought it was the Kool-1 starting to work, but it was too soon for that. No, it was Tif that made him feel that way.

A few weeks earlier Tif had been visiting Karen at their house. Brent was just getting out of the shower when he heard Tif calling to Karen, "I'll be there in a

toss, to throw, but not hard
gymnasium, a big room where sports can be played

second. I have to go to the little girl's room." When she walked into the bathroom and saw Brent, a big smile spread on her face. She took a couple of steps toward Brent, put her hand on the back of his head, and give him a big kiss. Tif didn't say anything, but left the room with a smile on her face.

Since that day, Brent had been waiting for a chance to talk to Tif. As he looked at her, dressed as a princess, Brent decided that tonight was the night. Billy continued to talk to him, but Brent couldn't stop himself from looking at Tif.

Several minutes passed, and suddenly Tif was looking toward Brent. He looked at her and a big smile came to her face. She said something to Karen and then walked toward Brent, still smiling. Brent took a deep breath and smiled back at her, as she got closer. When Tif was about two steps away, Brent took another deep breath – this time to say something to her. But Tif spoke first: "Hi, Trey," and walked right past Brent. He felt like the biggest idiot in the world.

Trey stepped away from Brent and the other boys and said something into Tif's ear. She looked up at him, smiled and shook her head. Then they both left the dance.

Brent wanted to scream. He couldn't stand the thought that Tif was with Trey. It felt as if rats were eating him up from the inside. But then the Kool-1 started to work and the feeling inside slowly went away. He looked around and saw Billy could feel the Kool-1 too. Other kids were starting to laugh a little harder, to dance more and to have a great time. Later the teachers would say it had been one of the best Halloween dances ever.

Thanks to Kool-1 Brent could no longer feel the rats eating his insides, but he did have a strong feeling that something was wrong.

Brent discovers something

While Brent and the other kids were having fun at their Halloween dance, youngsters in other towns were having a good time at their own school dances. At Root High School in Utica a number of kids had taken Kool-1 and were having fun. One of them, a boy named Bernie Culpa, was dancing with his girlfriend and suddenly fell to the floor. All of his friends laughed at first. They thought he was just being a *clown*. Bernie Culpa never got off the floor and was dead before the *ambulance* got him to the hospital.

Brent's father was reading the story of Bernie Culpa at breakfast on Monday morning. He asked Karen and

clown

ambulance, see picture, page 48

Brent if they had heard about something called Kool-1 at their school. Brent didn't know what to answer, but a voice in his head said, "Just say no," so he said to his father, "No." Karen kept her eyes on the piece of bread in front of her. Their father looked at both of them and said, "That's good."

A few other kids at school had been asked the same question by their parents. Billy was one of them.

"I was sitting there with five Kool-1 pills in my pocket when my mother asked me," Billy told Brent, as they walked toward school. "I just said no."

"I think you should stay away from that stuff for a while," Brent said. "A kid died from it."

"Ah, it's not going to hurt you. Anyway, they never said he died from Kool-1, but only that he had taken it," Billy said. "And even if it was Kool-1, it's like getting stung by a bee. Thousands of people get stung by bees every year and maybe one or two die from it. The kid was probably *allergic* to it. People can also die from eating food that you and I eat. Don't worry about it."

Brent really wasn't too worried. He was more afraid of getting caught with Kool-1 than he was of Kool-1 itself.

"I heard Jim Osgood's going to throw a party Saturday night," Billy said.

"I can't go. We're going to my grandmother's Saturday morning and won't be back until Sunday night."

As the week went by, some of the kids in school talked about the boy who had died. But on Saturday night, many of them would take Kool-1 at Jim Osgood's party.

allergic, when a person becomes ill from something he/she eats, touches, breathes

Brent and Karen had to get out of bed early to get ready to go to their grandmother's house. Karen was never really fun to be with, Brent thought, but in the morning she was like a tiger. He tried not to talk to her, or even look at her. On this day she was worse than ever.

"I don't know why I can't stay home. I'm almost 18," she said.

"You're not even close to 18," their father answered. "And you haven't seen your grandparents in a couple of months, young lady."

"Young lady!" Brent repeated with a laugh. Karen heard him and gave him THE LOOK. It was a look that could kill an elephant, but Brent just smiled at her. Karen was about to say something, but their father got between them. "All right you two. Let's get into the car, and I don't want to hear any more complaining."

Brent's grandparents lived in Montecello, around a three-hour drive from Port Mohawk. After they had been driving for around two hours, Karen asked, "Can I drive, Dad? Please?"

"I'll let you drive on the way home," he answered. Brent was half asleep, but he wanted to say something about Karen's driving. He opened one eye and was about to talk, but then closed it again. He chose to enjoy the peace while it lasted.

"Dad, I'm thirsty and I have to go to the bathroom. Can't we stop soon?" Karen asked. Brent opened an eye again to look at Karen. He wished she had stayed home.

"All right," their father answered. "There's a rest area just up the road. We'll stop there."

In a few minutes Brent felt the car come to a stop.

He opened one eye and saw a lot of parked cars around him. "Do you need to go inside?" his father asked.

"Nuunh," was all Brent could say.

"Do you want me to get you something to drink?" Brent was almost asleep and didn't answer his father. Suddenly he felt Karen's finger poke his ribs hard and his eyes jumped open. "Do you want something to drink!?" Karen asked. If Brent had had the strength, he would have grabbed Karen and held her down for hours until she promised to leave him alone forever. Instead, he took a deep breath, closed his eyes again and whispered, "Cola." Then he heard the two doors of the car close.

After a few minutes, Brent moved around in the car seat to make himself more comfortable. He opened one eye and looked out the window for a second before closing it again. Then both his eyes shot open. He was looking at Trey.

Brent moved lower into the seat so Trey wouldn't see him. Looking through the windows of a few other cars, Brent saw Trey getting into an expensive new car. Brent looked to see if Trey's parents were there, but they weren't. Trey was wearing clothes that were very different from what he wore to school. He normally wore nice clothes to school, but what he was now wearing were very expensive clothes. The leather jacket alone must have cost a couple of thousand dollars. Around his neck he wore two heavy gold chains and sunglasses covered his eyes. Trey sat in the car, started it and drove off. Brent sat upright and then got out of the car to watch Trey's car. The car drove onto the highway, getting smaller as it traveled further from where Brent stood. After a few seconds, the red right signal light began to blink and Brent watched as the car took the road that curved to the right. Then he noticed the sign: NEW YORK CITY – KEEP RIGHT.

Brent began to wonder about Trey. He thought about Trey and Tif together and it bothered him. But what bothered him was the way Trey looked, the clothes, the car. It was Trey, but it wasn't the Trey he knew – but then, he didn't really know Trey.

Brent could hardly think about anything but Trey all the time he was at his grandparents' house. He made up his mind that he would get some answers about Trey when he got home.

Pizza boxes

On Monday morning Brent went to school, but before the first bell rang he told Billy he was sick and was going home. As he was walking away Brent saw Trey and Tif kissing at one side of the school building. He felt the rats eating his insides, but he also felt an icy cold fear take hold.

Brent took his old bicycle out of the garage when he got home. He hadn't ridden a bike in a long time, but it was the only way to get there. The tires were soft, so he found a pump and pumped air until the tires were hard. Then he got on the bike and headed for Trey's house.

It was a long ride out to Steuben Road and most of it was uphill. Brent huffed and *puffed* for nearly an hour before he got to Steuben Road. He turned left onto Steuben and rode for another ten minutes before he saw a white house through the trees. The house was not close to the road, and Brent wasn't sure it was Trey's house, but it was one of the only houses on the road.

He got off the bike and hid it behind some bushes and walked slowly toward the house. Brent walked through the woods and tried to stay behind trees so he wouldn't be seen. When he was just a stone's throw from the house, he hid behind some bushes for a few minutes and watched the house to see if anybody was home. The *curtains* were drawn in all of the windows, so he couldn't see inside.

Brent couldn't see anything or anybody moving, so

puff, hard breathing
curtains, [kɔːtn] see picture, page 38

37

he decided to take a chance. He walked to the door and knocked three times. If anybody answered – maybe Trey's mother or father – Brent would ask where the Simpsons lived. He had never seen Trey's parents and they had never seen him, so there was little to worry about.

Brent waited and knocked again, but nobody answered the door. He knocked for a third time. Nothing happened, so Brent walked over to the garage. He looked through a window and saw a car. It was the same expensive new car he had seen Trey driving two days earlier. His skin felt like ice. Brent knew something was wrong.

He walked around the house, trying to look through windows, but the curtains blocked his view. Brent went to the back of the house, where he noticed an upstairs window just above the back *porch*. He saw the windows were the old kind, the same type that were in his grandparents' house. Brent got an idea from something he had seen his father do.

It was easy to climb onto the roof of the porch. Brent reached into a back pocket, took out his *wallet* and pulled out his library card. Around a year earlier he had

porch

been at his grandparent's house and his grandmother had locked the door, but had forgotten her keys inside. It only took Brent's father about two minutes to unlock a window with his credit card and get inside. "You should get new windows, Mom," he had said afterward, as he handed her the keys.

The window had two sections, an upper part and a lower part. It was made so a person could raise the lower part. Brent pushed the library card between the two sections and slid it sideways. He twisted and pushed the card against the lock, but it didn't move. He couldn't understand it, because it looked so easy when his father had done it. Brent tried again and saw the lock move a bit. He pushed and it moved a little more. In two seconds, the window was unlocked.

Brent looked around before trying to raise the lower part of the window. There were no houses nearby and all he could see was trees. So, he raised the window and climbed inside.

What Brent saw shocked him. He stood in an empty room. It had probably been a bedroom years ago, because there were four marks on the floor where a bed had once stood. There were three rooms upstairs and all were empty. There was *dust* everywhere and in some places there were footprints in the dust. Brent would have understood the rooms were empty even with his eyes closed, because the house had an empty smell. It didn't smell as if people lived there.

Brent looked around the three upstairs rooms and looked in all the *closets*. Nothing. So he headed downstairs. As he got halfway down the stairs his nose sensed another smell. It was a familiar smell, but Brent couldn't say exactly what it was. In a few seconds he found out.

Downstairs there was one large room, kitchen and bathroom. In the large room there was a bed that had been slept in. Brent realized what the smell was. All around the room there were pizza boxes on the floor. Some of them still had old pieces of pizza in them. A stereo was on one side of the room and there was a television right in front of the bed. There were no chairs, no table in the kitchen – none of the things a family had in a house, not even a refrigerator. It looked as if the person who lived here did nothing but eat pizza, watch TV and listen to music. In the kitchen there must have been a hundred empty soda bottles.

Near the door there was a big closet. Brent looked inside and almost fell over. The closet was full of clothes, enough clothes for ten people. The floor was covered with shoes and Brent recognized some of the clothes. On one side there were very expensive clothes and on the other side were the clothes Trey wore to school. They looked like the same kind of clothes all

dust, dirt
closet, small room where clothes or other things are kept

the kids wore, but the clothes hanging on the other side were different. On a hook next to the clothes hung ten gold chains. There was enough gold to buy a house.

Brent looked around. He didn't find anything, but then he really didn't know what he was looking for. He stood there looking around the room when a thought hit him. Upstairs! He remembered seeing footprints leading to one of the closets in an empty room upstairs.

He walked back upstairs and to the closet. It was easy to see that somebody had been using this closet for something. There was very little dust in front of the door.

Brent opened the door and stepped inside the closet. It was dark, but he could still see that the closet was empty. He stepped out of the closet and got out of the way so the light from the window would shine in the closet. At one corner of the floor there was no dust. Brent fell to his knees and felt the floor with his hands. There was a little hole between two of the floor boards. He put a finger into the hole and lifted the board, then lifted the one next to it. There was just enough light to see what was hidden under the floor. It was more money than Brent had ever seen in his life. Thousands and thousands of dollars tied together in square packages. Next to the money was a big bag of Kool-1. Brent reached down and lifted the bag and spotted something made of metal under the bag. It was a gun, and Brent decided it was time to go.

He replaced the boards and hurried back to the open window. Only after he had climbed out of the window and closed it did he realize that he couldn't lock the window again. Brent didn't care. He jumped down and raced to his bike.

Time to decide

It was around one o' clock when Brent got back home. He put his bike back in the garage and then went into the house. At first he thought about going back to school, but decided not to. He went to his room, lay on
5 the bed and started thinking.

Trey was not what he said he was. He wasn't a normal high school student. It was clear that Trey lived alone in the house. Where were his parents?, Brent wondered. That really didn't matter. What did matter was what he had found under the floor in the closet – a big bag of Kool-1, money, and a gun. And then there was the expensive car and all the clothes and the gold chains. Trey had arrived in Port Mohawk at the same time that Kool-1 had come. And he had all that money. Trey was the drug *dealer* who was selling Kool-1, and making a lot of money doing so.

But, Brent thought, he doesn't sell it and he doesn't take it either. He doesn't take it because he wanted to stay in control and take no chances, Brent figured. Then it hit him – Artie Flowers. Billy had told Brent how Janie Rolien dropped the Kool-1 as she would walk by. It was much safer than handing it to Billy, because if the police came she would say she didn't know anything about what lay on the ground. Artie used Janie so he wouldn't get caught and Trey probably used Artie so he wouldn't get caught.

Brent wasn't sure he was right, but it all seemed very simple. The big question now was, what to do? A week ago Kool-1 seemed like something fun to do. Now it seemed wrong in some way, especially after Brent had seen the gun.

He thought about calling the police, but didn't like that idea. For one thing, the police might not believe him and for another thing he might get Billy and maybe even himself in trouble. The same thing would happen if he told his father. And he couldn't tell Billy, because Billy might tell Trey and Trey had a gun. Karen? Forget about it.

Brent simply didn't know what to do. He thought for a long time and then decided that he would do

| *dealer*, seller

nothing. Trey had shown up in school one day, but he probably wouldn't stay there forever, would he? One day, Trey would simply disappear. They would come to school one day and his seat would be empty. Trey was a drug dealer and sooner or later he would know the police were getting closer to him, so he would simply move on to a new place. Brent believed what he was telling himself, but it was easy to believe because he was afraid of Trey.

Brent did make one decision – he would never take Kool-1 again.

The next day at school, Brent tried to stay away from Trey, but it wasn't possible. Trey was one of the guys. But Brent never tried to look Trey in the eye again. He didn't like what he saw in those eyes, and he was afraid Trey would see something in his own eyes. Trey seemed to have a way of knowing things.

Brent kept his secret to himself. One day, though, he said to Billy, "I think we should quit using Kool-1. It could be dangerous and probably killed that kid a couple of weeks ago."

"Don't worry, *dude*. It's not going to hurt you," Billy replied. "Anyway, I'm making too much money to quit now."

"You're crazy," Brent said. "Do you think you're going to become a big time drug dealer."

"I'm not a drug dealer! I sell something that makes people have a good time. That's all." Billy stopped for a few seconds. "Anyway, I won't be doing this forever. Right now it's kind of exciting, and I'm not hurting anybody."

| *dude*, guy

"It's your life, dude," Brent said. He wanted to tell him about what he had found at Trey's house, but stopped himself.

"You know what? You sound like one of the teachers or like somebody's father. They don't know anything about Kool-1, but they're all against it. All it is is something that makes people have a good time," Billy said. "And if you don't like it, don't do it anymore. But just leave me alone. I don't want to listen to anymore of your *whining*."

Brent watched as Billy walked away. For the next couple of weeks he didn't see much of Billy. They played basketball one Saturday and talked to each other in school, but things weren't the same. Billy was usually with Trey. Brent would often see him sitting beside Trey in his car as they drove around town. Brent was having a hard time keeping the secret about what he had seen at Trey's house to himself. He felt very guilty. It was not a good idea to just wait for the day when Trey would disappear. Brent thought about telling his father, but his father would just call the police. It seemed that all Billy was interested in was money. So Brent made a second decision. He would wait for a week and then call the police himself. Brent figured he could call from a pay phone. If the police asked him for his name he wouldn't give it to them. All he had to do was make a quick phone call, tell the police everything he knew and then hang up.

Brent believed that was a good plan, mainly because it was his only plan. He just hoped that nobody would get hurt by Kool-1 until he made the call and the

| *whining*, a crying complaint

police made the arrests.

One day Billy walked up to Brent and asked, "Are you going to Peggy Green's party on Wednesday?"

"Yeah, it sounds like it's going to be wild."

Peggy was one of Karen's friends, so most of the kids at the party would be older. Brent, Billy, Trey and some of the other kids in their class were also invited. Peggy's parents were going to her grandmother's for *Thanksgiving*, which was on a Thursday. They would be leaving Wednesday afternoon and Peggy would drive to her grandmother's on Thursday morning. Her parents didn't know that Peggy was planning a party, and she didn't want them to know.

"I can't wait until Thanksgiving," Billy said. "I need a few days off from school."

"Me too," Brent replied. It almost sounded like two strangers talking. Just a couple of weeks earlier the two of them would have been talking about all the fun they would have at the party.

"Just two more days ," Billy said.

The party

"Get out of the bathroom!" Brent yelled, and banged on the door. "You've been in there for more than an hour."

Karen just smiled at herself in the mirror.

"Dad!" Billy called. "It's almost nine o' clock. I have to take a shower and Karen's been in there for around two hours."

Thanksgiving, U.S. holiday for giving thanks, fourth Thursday in November

"KAREN," their father called.

After a few minutes Brent heard Karen unlocking the door. She walked out of the bathroom with a little smile on her face and didn't even look at Brent. "I have to make myself beautiful for the party."

"It didn't help much," he said, and hurried into the bathroom. He started to lock the door, but then remembered he had forgotten his shampoo. If he didn't hide his shampoo in his room Karen would use it.

The door to Karen's room wasn't closed all the way. Brent looked in. He saw her putting something into her mouth and then take a drink of water from a glass. She looked over her shoulder, surprised to see her brother looking in. Brent had been wondering whether Karen had ever taken Kool-1 and now he knew for sure.

"You're stupid," he said. Karen closed the door in his face.

Brent hurried to get ready for the party. He heard Karen call, "Bye, Dad," a few minutes later. It took Brent another half hour before he was ready to leave the house. He looked at his alarm clock and saw that it was almost nine o' clock. The party had started at eight, so he hurried all the more. "I'll see you later, Dad," he called, as he rushed out of the house.

While Brent was walking alone to Peggy Green's house, things were happening that would change his life. As he got to the corner of Larchmont Street – close to Peggy's house – an ambulance passed him with its red lights blinking. He didn't think anything of it, because there was no reason to. Brent walked on and in a few minutes he was at Peggy's house. Some other kids were standing at the door and he walked inside with them.

47

The music was loud inside Peggy's house and there were groups of kids in different rooms. Some of them were dancing, some were talking and laughing. Brent looked around to find some of his friends, but before he spotted any of them Tif Creetan grabbed his arm. Tif was still wearing her jacket, as if she had just gotten there, and she looked very upset.

She pulled Brent into a room where a few of Karen's

other friends were standing. All of them looked upset and a couple of them were crying. Brent looked around hoping to see Karen, but didn't see her.

"Brent ..." Tif started. "Karen has been taken to the hospital." Brent heard Tif's words and remembered the red lights of the ambulance a few minutes earlier. "We were walking along and all of a sudden Karen said she didn't feel well," Tif continued. "She said her heart was beating too fast ... and then she fell to the sidewalk. I called an ambulance on my cell phone."

Brent's own heart began to beat too fast. "Is she ...?

"Maybe you should call your father and get to the hospital," Tif said.

Brent's body started to shake as he looked around for a phone. "Here, you can use mine," Tif said, handing him her phone. "And Robin can give you a ride to the hospital." Tif, Robin and Brent hurried out of the house and got into Robin's car. Brent called his father as they started to drive. Inside the house, Karen's friends were telling other kids what had happened to her.

After he had called his father, Brent asked Tif and Robin. "Have you taken Kool-1, too?" Tif didn't answer, but Robin said, "I didn't, but ..." She reached into her pocket and took out a blue pill. Robin then rolled down the window and tossed the pill out.

It took them around ten minutes to get to the hospital. As they got out of the car, Tif said, "I'm going to wait here. I don't want to ... well, ah ... they might start asking questions and I'm a little afraid they'll find out I took it too." Brent was already inside the building, but Robin told Tif she would go in with Brent.

Brent looked around for a second and saw a sign: EMERGENCY ROOM and he followed the arrow. He came to a desk where a doctor was talking to a nurse. Brent read, 'Dr. Stiger,' on the name tag as the doctor spoke. " ... the heart begins to beat very fast, in fact, the heart races. But it beats so hard and fast that it doesn't get blood out to the body. She wasn't getting blood to her head, and that's when she lost consciousness."

"Doctor? Nurse?" Brent started to say.

"Just a minute. I'll be right there," the nurse said, holding up a finger. She turned to the doctor and asked, "Will she be all right?"

"The ambulance got there quickly," Dr. Stiger replied. "I only hope it got there on time. If the brain doesn't get *oxygen* then ..." Brent listened as the doctor said a lot of words he didn't understand. "We've done all we can for now. All we can do now is sit and wait, and hope," Dr. Stiger continued. "Have you called her parents?"

"I'm going to do that now," the nurse answered. "I got the girl's phone number from a card in her bag." She picked up the phone and said the numbers as she pushed the buttons. "Seven, nine, seven ...." Brent listened and suddenly his legs felt as if they couldn't hold him. The nurse had just dialed his phone number.

"It's my sister!" he cried. Dr. Stiger stopped what he was doing to look at Brent. "I've called my father. He'll be here soon." The nurse put down the phone, but picked it up again a second later. This time she called the police.

Dr. Stiger took a couple of steps toward Brent. "How long has your sister been using drugs?" he asked.

Brent answered honestly. "I didn't know she did

| *oxygen*, the part of air that we need to stay alive

until tonight." He felt somebody touch his arm. It was Robin.

"What about you?" Dr. Stiger asked.

Brent looked at his shoes for a few seconds and Dr. Stiger knew the answer to the question.

"Is she going to be all right?" Brent asked.

"I've done all that I can. She's still *unconscious*. We won't know for sure until we can do some tests later."

Just then Brent's father came up to them. Brent hugged him as hard as he could. Jim held Brent and asked the doctor questions at the same time. Dr. Stiger told Jim the same things he had told Brent, but said to Brent, "The police may want to ask you some questions later."

The nurse led Brent and his father to a waiting room. Robin followed them. "We have to take care of some things, but you should be able to see your daughter in a little while. We will move her upstairs shortly, and then you can see her," the nurse told them.

Brent fell into a chair and couldn't help but cry. He put his head down and the tears dripped onto his shoes. His father put an arm around his shoulder, and they waited.

Minutes passed, but Brent didn't raise his head. He couldn't look his father in the eye. "If only I had told him about Trey," Brent thought, over and over again. The words seemed to scream inside his head.

After a while Brent heard footsteps. He didn't raise his head, but could see a pair of black shoes and dark blue pants. He raised his head slowly until he was looking through his tears into the face of a policewoman.

| *unconscious*, [ʌnˈkɔnʃəs] not awake, knocked out

"Are you Mr. Scialfa?" she said.

Just then the nurse came into the room. "Mr. Scialfa, you can see your daughter now. Follow me."

Brent looked at the policewoman. She nodded her head to say that it was all right for him to go with his father. "But I'd like to talk to you later," she said, and then turned to Robin. "I'd like to ask you some questions." Robin had gotten to her feet, but sat down again. The policewoman sat beside her as Brent and his father followed the nurse.

When Brent walked into the room, he could hardly see that it was his sister lying in the bed. Karen had a mask over her mouth and nose, and tubes leading from machines to her arms. Her eyes were closed and the only sound was the Beep Beep of the machines, and a hhhhsshhuuuus sound as Karen breathed through the mask. Brent couldn't believe what he was seeing. He only wished Karen would jump out of the bed, so they could get into a big fight.

Brent and his father sat in chairs on either side of the bed. A long time passed before they spoke.

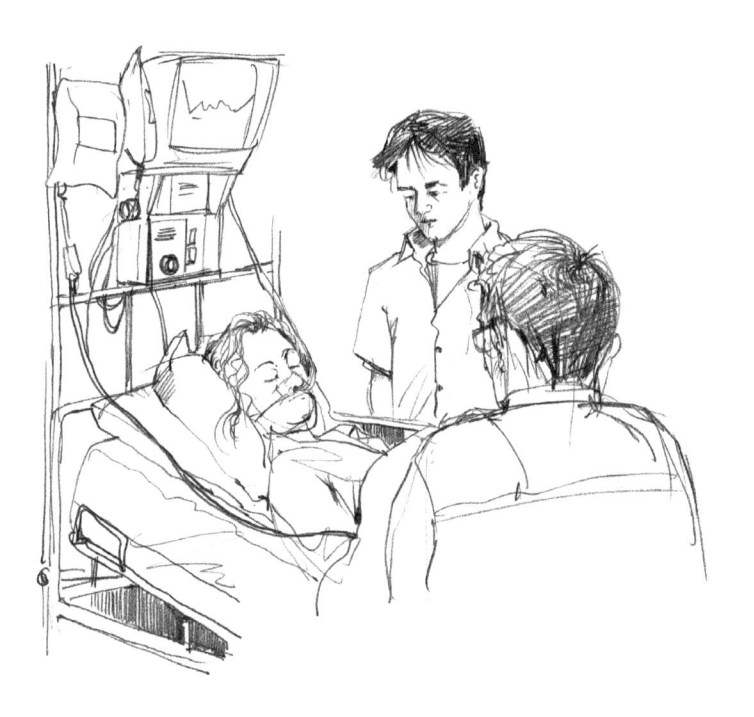

Trey takes Kool-1

Robin told the policewoman about everything. The policewoman made a phone call and a car was sent to Peggy Green's house where the police would ask more questions.

The kids at the party heard about Karen, but they never thought that it was Kool-1 that had done it. On top of that, most of the people at the party had taken Kool-1 themselves, so they were having a good time. There were some of the girls who worried about Karen, but most of the kids at the party were busy having fun.

Billy was sitting with Trey in the kitchen when the

police came to Peggy Green's house. The two of them were talking and drinking sodas as two policemen walked to the door and rang the doorbell. Billy had taken his Kool-1 a while earlier and was waiting for it to work. After a couple of seconds Billy and Trey heard someone shout, "The police!"

Trey got out of his chair and walked into another room to see what was happening. A lot of the other kids were running around. They were trying to hide the beer that some of them were drinking. A few kids ran into the kitchen and poured beer down the sink, while others took the empty cans and bottles and put them in the garbage.

When Billy saw the two policemen in blue, he got very scared. He still had around ten Kool-1 pills in his pocket. Billy had already sold a lot of pills, but he had taken more than enough for the party. He didn't know what to do so he pulled the pills out of his pocket and dropped them one by one into a can of soda.

The loud music stopped. A few of the boys came running into the kitchen and out the back door. The music stopped and Trey walked back into the kitchen. "I'm going to get out of here," Billy said to him.

Trey had faced the police before. He grabbed Billy's arm. "Just be cool," he said. "If you run from a lion the lion will think you're food and chase you. It's the same with the police. Just be cool."

Billy nodded, but the fear showed in his face. He walked to the door of the kitchen and looked into the living room where the police were standing. The two policemen were talking to a circle of kids. Billy listened and heard one of the officers say the word "drugs." The kids in the circle shook their heads to say no, or lifted their shoulders to say, "I don't know." Billy's heart beat fast. He was afraid one of the kids he had sold Kool-1 to would give the police his name. Billy tried to be cool, as Trey had said, but it wasn't easy.

Trey sat in a chair and was cool as ice. He lifted a soda can and drank from it.

Billy watched as one of the policemen walked over to talk to another group of kids. Both policemen were looking into kids' eyes. It was easy to see the ones who were on Kool-1 – their eyes seemed to be lighted up and they couldn't stand still. Billy watched as the police asked questions, and he had a hard time standing still. Trey sat behind him drinking soda. "Dude, be cool," he said to Billy. "They can't do anything unless they find something."

"I got rid of it all," Billy said over his shoulder, without looking at Trey.

Billy took a couple of steps into the other room. He didn't want to be standing alone and wanted to get closer to other kids. It felt as if the police would spot him more easily if he stood alone. Trey stayed in his chair. He lifted the can to his lips and downed the soda. The can made a clinking noise as Trey tossed it into the garbage.

Billy couldn't stand still, so he walked back into the kitchen. A second later, one of the policemen entered the kitchen. "Is your name Billy Falk?" he asked. Billy felt his face burning and nodded. "I'd like to ask you some questions." The policeman moved his head to tell Trey to leave the room. Trey stood up slowly and left the room.

"Have a seat," the policeman said and Billy sat down.

Billy looked around as the officer sat beside him. He moved his eyes to look at the can where he had put the Kool-1 pills. It was gone! Billy's heart began to beat even faster, both from fear and from Kool-1. He knew the police hadn't taken the can. "What happened to it?" he thought.

"You have a big problem on your hands, Billy," the policeman started. "But if you're willing to help us, then we can help you."

Billy tried to answer the questions without telling the policeman the whole truth. It didn't take the officer too long to figure out that Billy was the person the police were interested in. The policeman blew out a loud breath, waited for a few seconds and then said, "I think you'd better come with us. You can call your parents from the police station."

Billy walked ahead of the policeman into the other room. Trey was sitting in a chair in one corner, as cool as could be. The one policeman who had been questioning Billy nodded his head to his partner as if to say, "We've got our man."

Billy turned to the policeman. "Can I get my jacket from the kitchen?"

"Yes, I'll come with you."

As they left the room, Billy heard the other policeman say, "All right, kids, the party's over. You can clean up the house, but we'll be back in around an hour just to make sure you've all gone home."

Billy put on his jacket in the kitchen. As he did so, he looked around the room for the can of soda with the Kool-1 in it. He couldn't see the can anywhere.

Kool-1 wins

Brent and his father sat beside Karen's bed for nearly an hour before either one of them could say anything. They watched as Karen's chest rose with each breath, and then slowly fell. With each breath, they wondered whether it would be her last.

Finally Jim asked, "What happened, Brent?"

Brent didn't want to tell him the truth, but he looked at his sister once again. The sound of her breathing and the look on her face made him begin to talk. He told his father all about Trey.

As Brent was nearly finished with the story, a nurse walked into the room to check on Karen. She looked at the machines and wrote something down on a paper. Jim Scialfa looked at the nurse, hoping to hear good news. "We still won't be able to do any tests for a couple of hours," she said. "Why don't you and your son get a cup of coffee or a soda. There are some machines just down the hall. I can show you where."

They followed the nurse out of the room and to a waiting area where there were some machines that sold coffee, soda and other things.

"If there's any change, we'll come and get you," the nurse said. She shook her head. "Drugs are a terrible thing. We got another young person in here just a few minutes ago. This one wasn't so lucky."

Brent and his father really didn't care who the peson was. All they wanted was for Karen to wake up again and be herself.

But it was Trey who was in a bed in another room of the hospital. He had waited at the party for a few minutes after the police had gone. Then he got into his car to go home. Before he started the car, he took out his cell phone to call Artie Flowers. He wanted to warn Artie that the police would probably be paying him a visit. But before Trey could finish pushing the numbers on his phone, the Kool-1 hit him. And it hit him hard.

A couple of kids were leaving Peggy Green's house when they looked into Trey's car parked up the street. Trey's head was on the steering wheel and he wasn't breathing. The kids called an ambulance.

Dr. Stiger called another doctor to help when Trey arrived at the hospital. They worked on him for more than an hour. Then all they could do was use machines to keep Trey alive.

Brent drank soda while his father sipped a cup of hot coffee. They talked about Karen. Brent never knew he had so many good things to say about her.

They finished their drinks and went back into Karen's room where they talked some more. Both of them said things to Karen, hoping she could hear them and hoping it would help her to wake up.

They spent the night sitting by Karen's bed and going out to get something to drink every once in a while. At one point, Brent looked at the clock on the wall and saw it was six o' clock in the morning. It was just after six that the police let Billy go home with his parents. Billy had told the police everything, about Artie Flowers and about Janie Rolien. The police picked up Artie and found more than one thousand Kool-1 pills in his place. Another police team visited Janie Rolien's house, but they didn't find anything there.

At just after seven o' clock, Karen started to make some noise. "Ohhhhhhhhhhhhh." The sound came through the mask over her nose and mouth. At first Brent thought his father was making the noise. Then he saw Karen's eyes open a bit. "Dad," he cried.

Jim saw his daughter's eyes open once and close. "Go get a doctor or a nurse."

Brent rushed to find a nurse or doctor. He saw a nurse walking the other way and called to her. It was not the same nurse they had been talking to. This was a new face, a nurse who had just come to work early in the morning. "Nurse, my sister. Something's happening."

The nurse followed him into the room. She checked

the machines, felt Karen's hand then her head. A little smile appeared on her lips. "She's coming out of it," she said to Brent's father. "It's a good sign, but we still need to do some tests. I'll call one of the doctors."

Brent's father fell into a chair and covered his face with his hands.

A few minutes later the nurse returned with a doctor. Brent saw another person standing by the door. It was a policeman. Brent knew why he was there, so he went to the officer.

Two men in white clothes came into the room and rolled Karen's bed out of the room. "We should be finished in less than an hour," the nurse said, and followed the bed.

"Mr. Scialfa, I'm officer Petrucci. I'd like to speak with your son. Would that be OK?" Jim nodded his head. "You can join us if you like," the officer said. "Let's go down the hall and get a cup of coffee."

Jim bought two cups of coffee, but Brent said no thanks to another soda. The three of them sat down, Brent between the two men. Brent began to tell his story, but when he mentioned Trey's name, the officer stopped him. "That's the kid they brought in here earlier." Brent looked at the officer, then at his father, then back at the officer.

"What happened?" Brent asked.

"The same thing that happened to your sister," the policeman answered. "Only he wasn't as lucky as your sister. The kid's going to be like a stone for the rest of his life. His heart was stopped for several minutes. He'll never walk, or talk, or move again." The police officer continued to talk and said a long word Brent had never heard. It sounded like the name of a medicine, but had an idea of what it meant.

"Do you mean Kool-1?" Brent asked.

"Is that what you kids call it?" the officer said. "It has a lot of names, but it's still the same thing. A killer."

They were interrupted by the sound of footsteps. A doctor stood before them. He wasn't smiling. "Mr. Scialfa, your daughter is going to be all right," he said. "We'll have to keep her here for a couple of days, but the tests were all positive. She doesn't have any brain *damage*."

Kool-1 cools down

Karen came home two days later and Brent was happy to have her there. They only got into one little fight on the day she came home.

The police came to visit Brent once again a few days later and the newspapers were full of stories about Kool-1. Trey's name wasn't in any of the articles, but there was a picture of the Kool-1 and the money Brent had found in the house. There was also a picture of Artie Flowers in *handcuffs*, and the newspaper said that Artie would be going away for a few years. The stories

handcuffs

| *damage*, ['dæmidʒ] harm or hurt a person or thing

mentioned other people who had gotten picked up by the police, but did not give any names. Brent heard at school that the police had taken Janie Rolien, but let her go again because they did not find any Kool-1 at her place. Nobody said so, but Brent was sure that Billy had given the police Janie's and Artie's names. He was happy that he had done so.

Most of the kids at school stopped taking Kool-1. There were a few who still did, but very few. Brent wondered about other kids at other schools. He remembered how he and his friends had read about a boy who had died from Kool-1. They had thought about it at the time, but it didn't stop them. Kids in other towns must have read the newspaper stories telling about a girl who had almost died, and about a boy who would have to lie in bed without a brain for the rest of his life. Brent figured kids would read the stories, or hear them, and think that it could never happen to them.

Billy didn't come back to school for a whole week after the party. Some people at school heard that he had been sent away to a special school. It wasn't true. Billy had told the police everything and they let him go. But Billy was very scared for a few days.

The first two days he was back at school, Billy tried to stay away from Brent. Billy had sold the Kool-1 pill that had almost killed Karen, his best friend's sister. One day the two of them walked out of school and bumped into each other. Neither of them knew what to say. Billy wanted to run away, but his legs wouldn't move. Brent had so many feelings inside him, that he couldn't talk.

"Brent, I'm sorry," Billy finally said.

Brent waited several seconds before answering. "I

know, Billy," he answered. "I was very angry and never wanted to see you again. But then I started thinking. I took Kool-1, too, so I'm really no better than you."

"But you told me to stop and I didn't listen."

"Yeah, but you see, I knew all about Trey and I didn't tell anybody about it. That was stupid!" Brent said, and told Billy about how he had gone to Trey's house.

"So it was Trey all the time and not Artie Flowers," Billy said. "And Trey never took Kool-1, except that one time."

"I never really understood that. Why did he choose that night to take it?" Brent wondered.

The two of them walked along together without talking until Billy said, "The police took me to see Trey. They asked me about Trey and Kool-1 and whether I had ever bought any pills from him. I said no, and that was the truth. But I think they wanted me to see him."

Brent waited for an answer. Billy walked along looking up at the trees, trying to find words. "It was terrible, Brent. Trey lay in a bed and couldn't move. His eyes were open, but there was nothing in them. It smelled so bad in there, I couldn't stand it. I'll never forget the smell." Billy stopped and looked up at the trees again. He shook his head and continued: "The police told me they had to do something for a minute and asked me to wait in Trey's room. They left me alone in there. I didn't know what to do. I couldn't talk to him. All I could do was stand there and watch him. He was more dead than alive."

"Hey, take it easy," Brent said, touching Billy's shoulder. "Things will be all right from now on."

"You don't understand," Billy said. "Seeing Trey was

bad and the thought of going to *jail* scared the life out of me, but the worst thing was Karen. I felt that it was my fault. It was my fault. The police told me it was the Kool-1 that had put her in the hospital, but nobody told me until four days later that she was all right. I spent most of the time in my room or talking to the police. When I found out she was going to be OK, I wanted to call you and tell you how sorry I was. And call her too."

"Billy, I don't blame you. Well, I did for a while, but then I started thinking," Brent said. "We all had a choice to make. A lot of us chose to take Kool-1. We could have chosen not to."

"But I sold it."

"Yeah, you sold it, but if you hadn't sold it Trey would have found someone else who would," Brent said. "It's over now. At least it's over for us. Trey's gone, but I don't think Kool-1 will disappear now that he's gone."

They walked together for a few minutes, but were interrupted when they heard the sound of a car horn. Billy and Brent looked up and saw a new expensive car going slowly by. Janie Rolien sat behind the wheel. She looked right at Billy with a smile on her face. Janie put two fingers to her red lips, kissed them and blew the kiss at Billy.

jail, prison

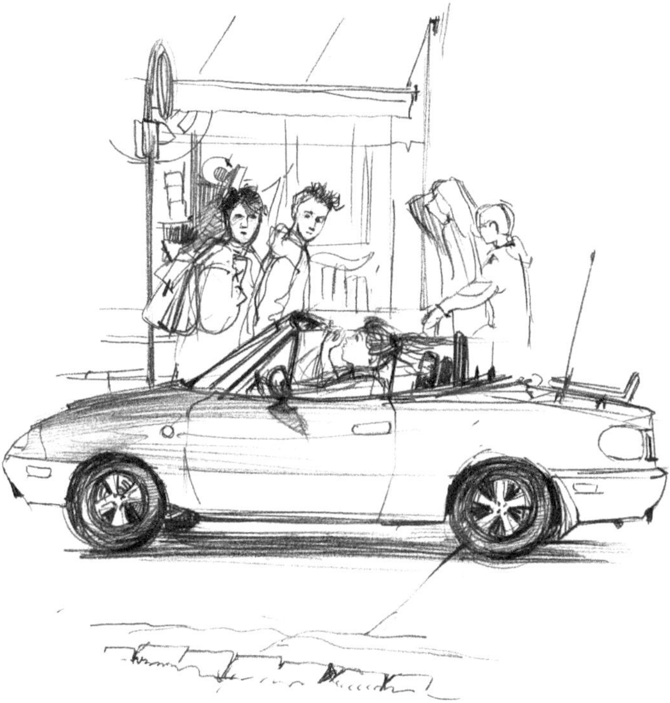

Questions

Who does Brent live with?

How did Brent meet Billy?

Do Karen and Brent get along like brother and sister?

Tell something about Trey's childhood.

Why did Trey go to Port Mohawk?

Did the kids at the new school like Trey? Why?

Why did Trey buy a second car?

Tell something about Artie Flowers and his place.

Why did Billy take Kool-1 the first time?

What happened at the Halloween party?

Why did so many kids take Kool-1?

How do Brent and Billy react when they learn a boy died from Kool-1?

Why did Brent decide to go to Trey's house?

How does Brent get into Trey's house?

Describe the inside of Trey's house.

What does Brent find in Trey's house?

What does Brent decide to do after he knows about Trey?

What would you do?

What happens to Karen?

Why do the police come to the party?

Do you think kids would still take Kool-1 after what happened to Karen and Trey?

Are drugs a big problem?

Why do kids take drugs?

How can it be stopped?

www.easyreaders.eu

NOTES: